W9-BFC-116

A Short History of
CHRISTMAS

by Sally Lee

Consulting Editor: Gail Saunders-Smith, PhD
Consultant: Jeannine Diddle Uzzi, PhD,
Director of Faculty Programs,
Associated Colleges of the South

CAPSTONE PRESS
a capstone imprint

Pebble Plus is published by Capstone Press,
1710 Roe Crest Drive, North Mankato, Minnesota 56003
www.capstonepub.com

Library of Congress Cataloging-in-Publication Data
Lee, Sally.
  A short history of Christmas / by Sally Lee.
     pages cm.—(Pebble plus. Holiday histories)
  Includes bibliographical references and index.
  ISBN 978-1-4914-6095-5 (library binding)—ISBN 978-1-4914-6099-3 (pbk.)—ISBN 978-1-4914-6103-7 (ebook pdf)
1. Christmas—Juvenile literature. I. Title.
  GT4985.5.L44 2016
  394.2663—dc23   2015002027

Editorial Credits
Erika L. Shores, editor; Bobbie Nuytten, designer; Kelly Garvin, media researcher;
Lori Barbeau, production specialist

Photo Credits
Alamy/Lebrecht Music and Arts Photo Library, 13; Corbis/Bettman, 7; Getty Images/Popperfoto, 9; iStockphoto: andresrimaging, 5, ferrantraite, 21, Juanmonino, 17, TonyTaylorStock, 15; Mary Evans Picture Library/Illustrated London News Ltd., 19; Shutterstock: Dragon Images, 11, Fears, cover (stockings), Karen Grigoryan, cover, xenia_ok, cover (illus)

Design Elements: Shutterstock/demonique

Note to Parents and Teachers

The Holiday Histories set supports national curriculum standards for social studies. This book describes and illustrates the holiday of Christmas. The images support early readers in understanding the text. The repetition of words and phrases helps early readers learn new words. This book also introduces early readers to subject-specific vocabulary words, which are defined in the Glossary section. Early readers may need assistance to read some words and to use the Table of Contents, Glossary, Read More, Internet Sites, Critical Thinking Using the Common Core, and Index sections of the book.

Printed in the United States of America in North Mankato, Minnesota.
042015   008823CGF15

Table of Contents

About Christmas

It is December 25. Today is
Christmas Day. We sing,
open presents, and talk about
Santa Claus. Let's learn
the story behind this holiday.

Before there was Christmas,

the Roman people had Saturnalia.

The December festival lasted

one week. People played games with

marbles, ate, and gave presents.

Two thousand years ago Mary
and Joseph went to Bethlehem.
Mary gave birth to Jesus Christ there.
Christians follow his teachings.
They honor his birth on Christmas.

Since the 300s Christmas has been on December 25. Church leaders chose the date. They wanted Christmas to take the place of other December festivals.

Saint Nicholas

Saint Nicholas lived in the 300s. He loved children. Some countries celebrate Saint Nicholas' Day on December 6. Children open presents from Saint Nicholas.

The Dutch people were the first to bring Saint Nicholas' Day customs to America. *Sinterklaas*, or Saint Nicholas, became Santa Claus.

Carols and Trees

Long ago people sang carols at happy events. By the 1100s people sang them mostly at Christmas. Many of today's favorite carols were written in the 1700s and 1800s.

Germany had the first decorated trees. In 1848 people saw England's queen and her German husband with a Christmas tree. The trees soon became popular everywhere.

Christmas Today

Christmas is a joyful time.
Today families open presents
together. Some people go
to church and sing carols.
People help those in need.

Glossary

carol—a joyful song sung during the Christmas season

Christian—a person who follows the teachings of Jesus Christ

custom—the usual way of doing something

decorate—to add things to make something prettier or stand out more

Dutch—having to do with the Netherlands, a country in Europe

festival—a celebration that is held at the same time each year

holiday—a day on which work, school, or any regular activities are officially stopped

honor—to give praise or show respect

popular—enjoyed or liked by many people

Roman—having to do with Rome, a city in Italy

Saturnalia—an ancient Roman festival honoring Saturn, the Roman god of agriculture (farming)

Read More

Frisch, Aaron. *The History and Traditions of Christmas*. My First Look at Holidays. Mankato, Minn: RiverStream Publishing, 2013.

McGee, Randel. *Paper Crafts for Christmas*. Paper Craft Fun for Holidays. Berkeley Heights, N.J.: Enslow, 2013.

Trueit, Trudi Strain. *Christmas*. Rookie Read-About Holidays. New York: Children's Press, 2013.

Internet Sites

FactHound offers a safe, fun way to find Internet sites related to this book. All of the sites on FactHound have been researched by our staff.

Here's all you do:

Visit *www.facthound.com*

Type in this code: 9781491460955

Check out projects, games and lots more at
www.capstonekids.com

Critical Thinking
Using the Common Core

1. What is a custom? Name one or two customs described in the text. (Craft and Structure)

2. Compare the photographs on pages 5 and 15. How are the two men the same? How are they different? (Integration of Knowledge and Ideas)

Index

Word Count: 223
Grade: 1
Early-Intervention Level: 18